Marrying the Sea

Other Works by Janice Kulyk Keefer

Poetry
White of the Lesser Angels

Fiction
The Paris-Napoli Express
Constellations
Transfigurations
Travelling Ladies
Rest Harrow
The Green Library

Criticism
Under Eastern Eyes: A Critical Reading of Maritime Fiction
Reading Mavis Gallant

Marrying the Sea

Janice Kulyk Keefer

Brick Books

CANADIAN CATALOGUING IN PUBLICATION DATA

Keefer, Janice Kulyk, 1952–
Marrying the Sea

Poems.
ISBN 0-919626-97-1

I. Title.

PS8571.E435M37 1998   C811'.54   C98-931284-4
PR9199.3.K43M37 1998

We acknowledge the support of the Canada Council for the Arts for our publishing programme. The support of the Ontario Arts Council is also gratefully acknowledged.

Cover images are after sculptures by Gilda Oliver, reproduced with the kind permission of the artist.
Photography is by Mickey Castle.
The author photograph is courtesy of Ruth Kaplan.

Typeset in Ehrhardt.
The stock is acid-free Zephyr Antique laid.
Printed and bound by The Porcupine's Quill Inc.

Brick Books
431 Boler Road, Box 20081
London, Ontario, N6K 4G6

e-mail: brick.books@sympatico.ca

For Branko Gorjup and Francesca Valente

sans pareils

Contents

I.

Sacra Conversazione

Sacra Conversazione

for Jane Magrath

In some open place
– poplars, a stream –
virgin, child and saints converse.

Faces turn in to one another, hands curve
to hold speech so clear
we hear it as silence.

But what of us, here,
where there's too much noise
for our voices to carry,

where language becomes a cloth
full of holes, or handkerchiefs tricked
from magicians' sleeves?

Poetry – a way of making
sacra conversazione. No borders
between lips and ears; a dance

of stillness, sounding
what we most desire: the eloquence
of dreams, that open dark

where we speak with the lost
or absent or dead. Speak with ourselves,
the winds gusting through us.

Alone in the Night

for you have spread out your night
over the pure gold of my Kremlin itself
and have tightened my throat with the pleasure
of singing   as if with a strap
        – Marina Tsvetayeva, *Poems for Akhmatova*

Returning to Yelabuga,
you looked up
to find no hills, no help

only the door you entered by;
a lintel from which
to hook a rope.

Pulling the loop over your head, did you remember
how a child's head crowns in birth, spurting
like silk through a ring?

Did you think to turn yourself
inside out – your body's worn dress
given back its sheen?

Lover of night, the green candles
of winter's sky, you who were always outracing
breath itself:

did you leap through that door, into
your city of forty times forty churches,
the steeled throat of their bells?

Oranges

for my mother

You were born with a craving for sugar
where kisses were rare as money.

It was a hard country, not like this one;
hunger wasn't something out of the Brothers Grimm.
Barely enough flour to make each day's black bread;
oranges something the priest alone enjoyed,
like holiness. He'd carve the peel into a star,
hang it with the icons on his wall. Longing
to know the taste of oranges, you broke off
a star-point, pressed it to your tongue.
Oranges, you learned, taste of dust.

Once you stole into the larder,
ate five packets of sugared baking powder
so that your belly swelled like a pumpkin and your face
turned a delicate, dead blue. Once
you took a straw from the barn and sipped
the cream saved for your saint's day – each day
a little more, until the bowl broke from its emptiness,
and your mother beat you.

There were always beatings in that country;
the sky must have been the colour of bruises.
It was necessary, you say – how else
to learn that scythes slice through the legs of children
sleeping in harvest fields; that the river was no deep,
cool hiding place, but a border
where guards shot to kill?

Those beatings I can understand,
the back of love's hand. But that boy
struck with a shovel till his spine cracked,
and no matter how many herbs, how many
healing baths he took, it hurt too much for him to ever
stand up straight again. Once, coming home from school,
you spoke kindly to him while the others
jeered. And after, a whole winter of waiting,
propped against his father's gate,
just to watch you walking.

The day you left for Canada, the whole village
came to see you off. He stayed at the gate,
hands jammed in pockets to keep
from falling, eyes tugging your sleeve
till you looked up –

did you know him, then:
the one who'd love you best?
Standing straight for you,
offering his pain, an orange

bloodsweet
through slashed peel.

Goat Stories

for Anna Simon

In your workroom, surrounded by sculptures,
making clay into the shape of your dead mother's face,
you tell me how your parents fled Poland for the Urals,
war scorching their backs at every stop.

What is the landscape of panic? Iron rivers,
skies cracked by flares, air
smelling always of ashes? The Urals –
I can't imagine that danger
called safety. Home a hut, walls blind with ice.

Your parents were put to forced labour, no one
to look after you but a nanny goat. She was warm,
she gave milk – your mother would leave you all day
tethered together. Searching the matted coat
you'd find a heartbeat – catch it
like a cricket in your hand.

The night you reached for milk warming
on the stove, soaked your hair in fire,
your mother ran with you in her arms
all the way to the hospital, tugging
the goat behind her. Into the white
carbolic glare, the rich smell of nanny goat.

The end of these stories
you had no part in making: 'And then one day
they ate her, my beautiful goat!
I couldn't believe it.'

Perhaps the goat had lost her milk,
grown too hard to keep – the neighbours forever
trying to turn her into their own
small sacks of meat. With country people,
animals are worked or eaten. Your parents, in those mountains,
had to be country people.

But Anna, the story doesn't end
with your nanny goat, eaten.
It's become your telling it, here,
in words or – like some hero in a fairytale –
through speech learned from the animals:

that heart, still spelling its heat
through your hands. Shaping
these burdened, running figures;
your mother's lost, lifted face.

Travelling

for Branko Gorjup

Now Freud says of the maternal body that 'there is no other place of
which one can say with so much certainty that one has already been
there.' Such then would be the essence of the landscape (chosen by
desire): *heimlich*, awakening in me the Mother (and never the disturbing
Mother).

    — Roland Barthes, *Camera Lucida*

This is what you have been told:
you were six or perhaps eight years old,
and your mother put you, alone, on a train.
That kind of thing was done then.
Nothing happened. The train left Zagreb
and arrived at Split on schedule. You stepped out,
your hair combed, your coat still fastened.
Relatives were there to greet you,
the weather was fine throughout your stay.

This is what you remember:
the train starting to move
while your mother is still embracing you.
The windows that won't open
though you see your mother fall,
the door from which strangers have to hold you
for the first few miles.
How the whole journey happens in a tunnel:
blackened glass, no fields or sky,
only your mother hurtling to the ground,
the pulp of her legs —

Much later you told her this
and she laughed saying, 'It was nothing –
I got a little shock, that's all; the pavement was harder
than I expected. But I brushed off my skirt and walked home.'

You left home long ago. Now a war
keeps you from returning to a city, a house,
a mother older than you'll ever know her. You,
a grown man, telling me this story
as if it were a shard of glass you've never let go,
braving again and again its raw kiss:

the shock of that leap you can never make,
back to the place where you were never parted.

Kyiv, 1995

for Maryna Bondarenko

We met at the airport, you were holding a sign, my name misspelled.
Driving in, we made a language between us: scraped bones of
  Ukrainian, dictionary English.

May, you said, was the time to visit Kyiv: chestnuts flouncing the
  Khreshchatyk, hiding
brute buildings, monuments to undying friendship between butcher
  and calf. This was
November, the trees held out empty cages. I never once saw sun.

That first night, eyeless lamp-posts, ragged streets, a park overlooking
  the Dnipro;
I had to make up the river from the lights of boats, stars thrown down
  a hillside.
Five days we walked your city: museums, mansions in powdered
  shades of Turkish delight.
Kiosks stocked with kings' ransoms – Campbell Soup, Johnny Walker.
Under the pavement, under the still-green grass, bones so deep the
  soil is white.

Something I must tell you: that day you took me to Pecherska Lavra,
walking a maze of mouths hollowed through clay, I saw you limping.
One whole day in and out of rain, chill of soaked umbrellas, I said
  nothing.
I hadn't the words, I had so little time, you never complained.

I'm writing to thank you, is there something I can send you?
You're just old enough to be my daughter, so young I can't trust my
  taste.

On my way over, I brought you nylons. Tea and instant coffee.
American dollars.
But you liked best my mother's cake, sweet jewellery of almonds, red
and green cherries.

Tell your mother I remember that dinner, table heaped with hours
spent queuing at food stalls,
toasts drunk in communion wine, endearments – your cousin,
rybochka, little fish.
After so much strangeness, that room, brave with books and paintings
– I felt at home there
till someone asked, *Your mother, is she glad she got out, would she ever
come back?*

If we spoke the same language could I ask, does it afflict you?
Porsches on gas-starved streets. Whole currencies of coupons
worthless in your desk.
And the river, licked by Chornobyl, irradiated leaves of chestnut trees.

Snow here, darker than we can remember. And you, your country,
that far room
in this wrecked house we share? Forgive me that wrenched walking,
our candles thinner
than a little finger, through those small white caves under the ground.

Stones

for Avril Harvey

You flew across oceans, continents,
time zones; years collapsed
like junked umbrellas

as you walked into her hospital room.
She already had a visitor: death,
doing one of his monologues

inside her skull –
a bowl to be sucked clean,
then stuffed with silence.

Thirty years of speech so close, you seemed
to share a room instead of distance.
Thirty years of long, densely-written letters.

So this is how it is, she said,
as you stood beside her. A clarity
not to be slurred by pity or grief.

These last words she gave you
small, heavy as stones. Something to hold,
something true that won't vanish.

You write all this to me, how years
and years of words compact:
this is how it is

sitting together
in the light clearness makes.
Just breath, while it lasts, between you.

along the lake

for Bronwen Wallace, 1945–1989

A freak, this warm mist blowing up
over the ice. Gray ice, the permeable
lace of bone.

This is the pathway of the dead.
Insouciant as angels they set out,
faces beyond recall,
eyes shedding everything but white.

No bird, no leaf to interrupt
the weightless language of this air. See
how they move where ground gives way,
the mist that buoys them

even as it stays us here,
holding out arms that won't dissolve
into the longing we extend:

bridges stronger than the thickest ice.

Dovedale

for Catherine Byron

Digging the garden, making room
for marigolds, nicotiana,
I think of you, an ocean away –

your paddock, abundant with lilacs,
wild thyme. Pruning sheers rusting
in a neglect like love, and the grass long
as your long, fine hair.

☙

Poems, letters threading
the zero of distance. The brush of your hand across a page.
Words shaped to the curve of your eyes,
the eyes of Van der Weyden's Magdalene,
no ascetic in a desert, but a woman lost in her reading,
abstracted from whatever larger scene
makes her a fragment.

This is what distance does – I lose
the skin of your stories, make do
with bare bones:

your *Catalogue of Illustrious Women* –
that Australian friend, greening the desert
with parsley watered from artesian wells; women
delivering themselves from dragon marriages; the ones
still sewn in a fortress of stitches, searching for scissors.

Or else mere catechism: what
your convent school taught you of puberty:

You will notice changes, girls,
mysterious changes in your bodies.
Q: *What sort of changes?*
A: *Your scalps will start producing oils,*
making your hair gleam, a crowning glory.

❀

Walking with you a year ago, in Dovedale – two days' talk
after as many years apart, making each fluctuation
of those unknown hills familiar as the tongue inside my mouth.

You named for me *wolfsbane, yellow archangel*. Found footholds in
limestone slick as a newborn. You walked those hills the way your
    poems
travel their pages: as though the map were traced on your bones.

And yet the risk, always: finding your way alone. Telling
how the very ground shifts – marriage stopped, children grown,
the pathways of your body turning transient as light.

❀

If it could always be this effortless, if we could always hold
speech. Hands cupped round words that pour away, the more
we drink. If you were here, now, I would tell you

how I can't write without tearing my nails.
The despair after making;
nothing ever good
enough, nothing true.

Or this suddenness of being bound to time,
my hands trapped like a clock's.
Each birthday a thief,
my body a house whose doors won't lock.

❀

Digging the garden, making room
for what, on this cold slope, might grow.
Crouched like a rusted penknife
over annuals, remembering
your unkempt lilacs, all the months
since we've written –

lackadaisical abundance
or a dying back? *Love*,
we sign our letters: charms against
the damage of *seldom*. Will we meet next
in the airport of emotion:
strangers in familiar dress
walking towards   then

                    unstoppably past each other?

Or will language save us,
joining us like runner roots?
At intervals, through dense silence –
bursts of shoots.

This earth I open like a clumsy surgeon:
all this webbed and living dark. These words
I send you: sunk,
small
migratory bloom.

Cedars

for Tom, 15

Late afternoon, light slippery.
You take me into the cedar woods,
the place you know best on earth.

Walking together, we're new
as strangers, no history
already shared. You show me
the forts you've made – a lean-to, an aerie;
root tapestries, boughs pushed
fragrantly through.

Less and less light. The cedars become
a shaggy maze, needing translation:
you help me over fallen trunks
the way I once helped you
when you were small enough to need
only a hand.

Who are you now, what will you make
of all that fearlessness inside you? Pushing
through the sudden dark, your eyes
clear as blades.

Horses

for Christopher

After you finally learned to read –
when words, instead of stamping, rearing,
came to lay their muzzles in your hands,

I'd take you the long way home from school,
past the neighbour's paddock. Pockets rich
with windfall apples, you'd run ahead

to that place where the air shook
with the violence of grass
torn live from its roots.

Two plush mares. And a pony,
a crouch-backed pony,
yellow teeth long as piano keys.

How the pony's bloodburst eyes
drew you. I could hardly bite down
my fear at your holding out

a small, scarless hand. Somehow
you knew how to keep the palm flat,
your fingers barely curved.

You never asked to ride, just stood
silent as the apples you slid
through the fence,

sharing that last unbroken
language, his tongue
roughing your hand.

Anaesthesia

When the self calls to the self, who answers?
    – Virginia Woolf

The poplars are cold, black eyes of their trunks
won't shut. Whatever the leaves say to the wind
frightens you, as if you were a child
hearing your parents fighting,
for the first time understanding *menace*.
Rain on poplar leaves, countless clear
blind eyes. That test they gave babies:
diamond-patterned floor, and a place
where the pattern sloped into a hole, glassed-over.
Strong, thick glass, but the babies stopped,
drew back, sensing the tricks
safety plays, how it's only a gloss on danger.

What's inside you that you cannot reach, ditch
thick with leaves now blown away?
Pain, that esperanto we all speak. Transpose it
into your own idiom: pain performed in that high-ceilinged office on
Queen Street, a building smelling
of dust and necessity. Pain on the stairway, in the varnish
on the door, Pluto's black handwriting: *Please Walk In.*
Jut of fluorescence, caustic in corners. And you
in the chair, your father sharpening picks
and shovels, mining the dark in your mouth.

What's the soil in which you grow, skeleton's
blind ripening? Child putting hands
to the breast, finding a crevasse:

I wish you'd never been born,
I should have strangled you in your cradle.
No love that doesn't sometimes
bite instead of kiss. Bite
the way animals do, to tear off flesh.

Say we're all set crawling at the lip
of an abyss. Some are glassed,
some are chutes like the dark flesh of the throat.
How many swallowed without sound,
for whom the word *pain* is meaningless, because
there's never been anything else? That boy the neighbours
watched dragging his bones up the front steps, neighbours thinking
something wrong with a child too weak
to open his own front door. Not knowing what they knew.

What of those others, who somehow
survive affliction – fists slammed up
tunnels that haven't dreamed
of opening yet? The unjust commonwealth of pain
which can conceive, but not imagine hierarchies:
that eight-year-old already punchdrunk
with his mother's jibes: *you useless worthless stupid* –
higher or lower than the child gagged for years in an attic,
lashed to a chair?

You survive. You grow up, grow over. If memory's
a garden, let it go to seed. A fine harvest
of scars, ground you can stand on, raising your children,
emptying their own bushels of fears.

You build a house in your head, architecture
of explanation: the migraines mapping your mother's head, intricate
archipelagos of pain. The child your father was, rushing from his
father's fists through a house too bare for hiding places.

You build a house, rent it out, board it up,
but suddenly the walls fall in,
pin you under. On examination
the doctor finds nothing broken, nothing
to account for your complaint: not pain

but utter estrangement from joy,
from taking or giving joy. As if inch by inch
you'd pulled on a skin of cinders, smoke clogging
even the whorls of your fingertips. Or that lead apron
they drown you with before clicking the ex-ray machine.

🐚

Some huge bird's flown inside me, claws
hooked into my ribs. It keeps beating
its wings, trying to leap
into a wind that isn't there,
beating and beating.

35

or

When I walk down the street, I make myself
go so fast, someone once called out,
'You look like a moving target.'

What lies under the glass floor? Walking out, now,
along its glimmer, what opens to you?

That tea-towel someone pinned to the wall,
a calendar of homilies: *I will pass*
through this life but once. No pain, no joy.

Forgive, and remember?
Forgive, and forbear? Learning
what trees do: disburdening,
then putting forth. Their rooted travelling, in seasons,
never entirely leaf or branch. So that winter's spine
prints through the skin of summer.

Late autumn. Evening.
Rain, not ice, splits the air. A throng
of poplars, trunks fleshed
as if they were naked, and breathing.

Wind voller Weltraum

All night, storms without rain or snow, just wind
whirling up and down tunnels,
endlessly moaning.

Corn husks blown as far as seven storey buildings.
A whole skeleton – trunk and spiked hair –
in the tilled figure-eights under the spruce.

Rilke's wind full of infinite spaces, up-ending
that table in the head, so neatly set.
This longing for sound, not shelter –

All night, wind blowing down the dark.
Ghosts crying in voices
insistent as oceans, unstoppable.

II.

Sirens' Songs

Sirens' Song

Come over, come over.
There's plenty of room on our island, lost
in the sea of your shouting, your great
humdrumming ears.

It's not our fault
you never learned to swim.
Make a raft, not excuses –
any old plank will do.

No stomach for singing?
We could talk, instead.
Tell you stories. You could even
ask questions, as long as they're not

the same old questions:
Busy tonight?
Marry me?
What do women want?

Look at your poor hands,
blistered with rowing,
your eardrums parched
for something finer than wax.

Come over, lie like
conch shells round us;
feed on the honey
we comb from our hair:

honey and fire. All divinity
is dangerous, and we were born
of Tragedy and a river god, a seethe
of salt and sweet water –

Birds, not bones
in the trees of our tongues:
birds in whose throats
your dead souls will sing.

Eurydice

while wandering with her nymphs, shortly after her marriage, was seen
by the shepherd Aristaeus, who was struck by her beauty and made
advances to her. She fled, and in flying trod upon a snake in the grass....

    – Bulfinch's *Mythology*

Silent, in Tempe,
the valley of the river Peneus. I was not
with my nymphs, I wanted no one's company.

Picking up stones from the river's edge,
stones marked with language
for which I had no alphabet. Swallows flashed warning

and I ran. All I could see
was the grass my feet interrupted,
a world of infinite divisions

and yet no hiding place. Except for a snake, quicker,
more agile than any shepherd. Smaller punctures,
a cleaner wound.

'O deities of the underworld ... I come to seek my wife, whose opening years the poisonous viper's fang has brought to an untimely end. Love has led me here ... I implore you by these abodes full of terror, these realms of silence and uncreated things, unite again the thread of Eurydice's life.'

Always someone chasing me, even
in Tartarus. No one thought
to ask –

I would have told how death
is a falling into earth like air.
How, as we walk in dark meadows
by the darker river,
nothing contains us.

The very stars seem closer; I can read
stones, shells, the warm sides
of animals – even the diamonds
on a serpent's skin are language. Here
our mouths unlock,
death's atmosphere a crystal rim
each newborn tongue sets ringing.

By the time he came for me
I'd forgotten the need for running.
My limp had hardened into me,
a root more intricate and rich
than petals on a bridal couch.

❀

Orpheus was permitted to take her away with him on condition that he should not turn round to look at her till they should have reached the upper air. Under this condition they proceeded on their way, he leading, she following, through passages dark and steep, in total silence till Orpheus, in a moment of forgetfulness, to assure himself that she was still following, cast a glance behind him, when instantly she was borne away.

At first he heard nothing, mistook my words
for the drip of water, stones falling
from cavern walls. But as we walked,
I kept on calling out to him. Not *wait*
or even, at the last, *farewell*,
but always, only, *listen*

the voice he would not recognize, the tongue
death opened into me.

When he turned I was already gone,
back to my river, my companions,
our talks about the flight of birds, of seasons:

fluctuating music of the spheres.

Orpheus ... held himself aloof from womankind, dwelling constantly on the recollection of his sad mischance. The Thracian maidens ... feeling themselves despised ... raised a scream and drowned the voice of his music. They tore him limb from limb, throwing his head and lyre into the river Hebrus.... Orpheus's shade passed a second time to Tartarus, where he sought out his Eurydice....

A tremor in the constellations.
Wherever I walked, someone was following me –
at a distance, burdened. At last I turned

and in the clear, black air saw Orpheus
carrying his head in his arms.
I went to him, put my hands to his eyes

the way you'd shut the door of a room
where someone you loved lay sleeping.
His bed is the river; long grass

bends over him. Dreaming
the silence of snakes, stones,
music only he can hear.

Mary Magdalene

Magdalen is the same as *manens rea*, remaining in guilt, or means armed,
or unconquered or magnificent.... For before her conversion she
remained in her guilt, being laden with the guilt of eternal punishment;
in her conversion she was both armed and unconquered ... because she
put on the excellent armour of penance, devising an immolation of her-
self to atone for each of the pleasures she had enjoyed; after her conver-
sion she was magnificent by the superabundance of grace, because where
sin abounded, grace did more abound.

   – *The Golden Legend*

My name is Mary, of Magdala,
though I'm known in these parts
as The Sinner. These parts belong to me:
this fortified town, its markets and temples
and taverns. My lineage is royal;
my parents are of noble station.

I am beautiful and rich
and literate. My clothes are exquisite,
my body gilded
and sugared and oiled.

Magdala is a terminally
dull town. I would rather live
by the sea, I would even rather pace
the desert than these streets with their coarse bloom
of fleece and flour. My brother Lazarus
gets by doing army drill: Martha,
my sister, has a head for business – all day
she chases coins up and down a ledger till

her feet ache; they sink her into night
like anchors. As for me,
I've had to go in for abandonment.

Abandonment is not what you think.
It was hard work, loosening my hair
that has never been cut, flinging open
all the doors of my body. A rash of scents
embroidered my skin; walking became
difficult, and I could barely speak,
my tongue worn thinner than a wafer.

I have had my pick
of every councilman and judge,
every merchant and physician,
poet and harpist, every soldier
and prophet passing through Magdala.
But I have never had anything
to say to them.

As for pleasure, that fat gold fish –
it keeps swimming farther and farther away
from my skin, my hair. It has found
some deep well in me: water
no one has ever drawn.

Tears must be the true abandonment.
If once I could find some cause to weep;
if only once through the streets of Magdala,

the bone-dry streets of Magdala,
a stranger would appear at a turret or behind
a garden wall, and summon the grief in me –

gladly I would kiss his open eyes,
and wash his feet.
I would follow him even

into a sea of sand. We'd lie
on the raft of my hair and feast
on fish and salt, forever.

Say it With Flowers

In the blue light of an iris
(which will not shrug off its sheath)
I am writing to you. What do you want to hear
at the other end of silence? Falling snow, the merest brush
against the ear, clean as white chocolate?

Why such extravagance of scent
in a season of stalks and husks?
Who do you think I am – somebody's lilac girl,
queen of the never-blooming May?

I'm hungry, and you send me flowers. I cannot eat
the iris – it has so little blood left its stem
no longer tarnishes the water. Freesia
already senile, withered trumpets always
sounding the wrong note. As for the roses,
they sag, and bloat.

You could have sent yourself,
brought hoe and spade and dug a garden;
instead you send these messengers, peg-legged,
signalling not love, but distance.

I've had to use the narrow-necked jug
because the iris has, indeed, died prematurely
and there aren't enough flowers left to fill
the hell-mouth of the crystal vase.
I have to endlessly adjust and re-arrange
just to keep space from gaping.

I'm tired now, and even hungrier.
Instead of flowers I would like to send you
kisses: dozens of sharp,
white bites.

My name is Red, and
I Can Tell You a Thing or Two About Wolves

1. No fangs, no claws:
   even the snakes of his throat –
   I thought they would squeeze me
   and squeeze me, but they're lazy,
   just like him. How his ribs shake
   between snores – the jolt
   of a subway car, shooting tunnels.

   No room in this belly for baskets, checked napkins,
   the accoutrements of being good. It's snug,
   it's warm, I like it here.
   No errands to run, no
   exclamations to make, and wherever I look
   I see red:
   dark, meaty, pumped
   through the heart.

   Over the rib-racket, my mother's voice,
   promising a whole wardrobe: red blouse,
   red petticoat, red
   bra and all accessories. I know
   what happens to girls wearing red shoes
   in this neck of the woods:

   I know all about wood-cutters,
   how they chop light
   into sky's black belly. Their steely
   hands, tugging me up
   by the soaked cord of my hair.

2. Now I live with mother and the wood-cutter
   in a house purged of all inflammatory shades.
   By day I eat sugar-cream without the strawberries,
   wear bleached muslin, *broderie anglaise*: clouds
   I tuck into bed each night before I steal
   into the woods.

   On a blade-bare bough
   a wolfskin hangs; I leap
   through the hole
   that was his mouth –

   deep in the salty grass we lie.
   With his long, long
   tongue, the wolf unties

   my cloak: each bow
   a blood moon
   a forest fire.

Plat garni

In a High Victorian painting by one of those indefatigable
wanna-be Greeks – Leighton, or Dodds –

three young blondes in tunics the tint of peach sherbet,
the consistency of peach sherbet as it froths your tongue,
are arranged upon a couch, reading. That is, blonde
number 1 floats the full length of the sofa,
anchored by a single elbow. Her hands are meringues
filled with a black-covered anachronism:
Petronius perhaps, or Sallust,
Loeb edition. She is reading aloud,
we infer, to numbers 2 and 3, their small
mouths shut yet secretly engaged,
as though sucking on peppermints.

This is a painting that may have hung
in the dining room of a men's club fabled
for blanc-mange and floating island. The women's hair
is the softly rumpled skin of angelfood cake;
their arms and necks and plump,
undimpled feet, the slightly saline
flesh of simmered shrimp.
They fit into their fluted tunics the way
parfait piles inside a long-stemmed glass:
exposed, yet closed away, making the tongue
voyeur.

Lounging, lolling, yes – but why
with book in hand? They don't seem to be reading
or listening with any gusto. There's something glutinous
in their expression, in the milky light
boiling over the canvas. Nothing so indelicate as lust, but
boredom easily mistook for languor, boredom
indigestible as rubber. The book, of course, is a prop,
its pages nothing but white sauce. Moreover,

these girls may well be hungry, and there's not even
a crust in sight. For want of nourishment they may have to eat
each other – slyly, of course, so the bites don't show. After all,
the painter's laid on skin to spare, and drapery enough
to cover multitudes.

Once they've finished with the menu,
the gents may find nothing
but bones to pick.

Degas' *Women on the Terrace of a Café, at Night*

I have bad habits, such as
sucking at my thumbnail. Claudie,
who always keeps her gloves on when doing business,
gives me the evil eye.
It's not attractive her eye says:
it won't exactly reel them in.
Claudie with her ridiculous hat, an *assiette*
de crudités slammed on her head.
At least I'm not scratching my back,
or yawning. I am bored.
Boredom is good for bad habits.

I would like to be home,
in my chemise, corsets crumpled
as candy wrappers.
I would like to be home
with Claudie without her hat
and her hatpin eye, the two of us
eating sticky buns,
roasting our feet by the fire.

We curl up against the cafés columns,
the pavement a thumb's breadth
from our skirts. If only
one of those men in rain-greasy top hats would stop,
signal, buy me a glass of wine
heated with lemon and a little cinnamon

he would see that my bonnet
and my striped mauve silk can't keep out
the chill of an April night. I'd give him my arm
and we'd stroll off under the giggling lamps.
By the time I got home there'd still be an hour
or two for sleep. And just when the waiters started
crashing dishes, Claudie would stumble out to buy
pain au chocolat. I'd feel the bed lurch;
pretend it was a train, headed for places
where the weather's bronze as brandy.

I sit with my eyes half-closed,
sucking at my thumb. I can just see Claudie's hand
in its black glove, opposite my elbow.
We seem to lean away from one another,
but our feet, in their stiff boots, touch.

Between us a table top
and a glass of absinthe,
pale morning.

Elizabeth Smart, 70

I have travelled so far
from the country of my birth
that my body's become a lunar Sahara.
In the craters of my eyes, light burns out
with the superb slowness of stars.
Remembering that girl, her hair soft as butter,
you say it hurts to look at me.

Look at the garden, then – I made it
out of a gravel dump, quarrying roses
like Carrara marble. If you want skin
without stitches, fresh-smelling involutions,
pay attention to the tuberoses, not to me.

I don't know why you're so mopey.
Look at my flowers, my children, their children:
look at my book – you carry it like a furled
umbrella, as if reluctant to remind me

that the Muses have whispered their milk
into my lips. Does this embarrass you,
the casual terms I am on with greatness?

I will remind you only once:
I want to be respected by those who are dead.
I want to sing and make my soul occur.

The first time I lit a cigarette, I was so nervous
I held it like a pen. For a while I wrote fire.
Now my eyes are blood and ashes:
no water can bring back their white skies.

He is dead, and I am nearly there.
What is there to talk about?
Come sit for a while in this garden;
the bees will astound you with their whisky hum,
and the snapdragons, that never stop
shutting up.

Katherine Mansfield to Middleton Murry

No mirror gives me back my face.
I lie alone, in a strange bed, my skin
all ears against my emptiness.
I have no language left. No one here
can pronounce my name. Everyone knows
I'm about to die.

Trams rush past like dry oceans, a telephone
rings and rings in another room.
Cover me with something warm. My lungs
are drinking my blood in gulps, soon
I'll be nothing but bones, soft, pale
as the marzipan pigs they sell for Christmas
in this city of locked windows.

When the doctor comes I stare into the eye
of his stethoscope. Do you understand what it means
to be alone? Sometimes I think
of the Christ Child in that stable,
stranded in radiance,
everyone worshipping and no one
picking him up.

I'd rather die in a barn than this hotel.
I want all the cows around me,
letting me drink their soft, wet breath:
milk from the teat, milk saying *we are with you,*
you are surrounded by love,
no harm can come to you.

My mother died long before I was born. My father
has left for the last time, giving me
some daisies and an orchid tied up
with grass. I have no child. Your work
keeps you in England, and as you say, the Riviera
is by far the best tonic for me, cheaper
than a sanatorium. I may even improve
for a while, I may even be able to write again.

Tomorrow will be better.
If not tomorrow, then the day after. You'll see,
I'll be through with this place long before
it's through with me. One day, I'll set off
with my notebooks and my pens,
my black cape prickling the grass –

I shall vanish into a motor car piled with cushions
high and rosy as the Alps. The driver will be
a trusted friend; there won't be a single road
down which we won't venture, a barn too rough
for us to sleep, bodies tangled
like the fringes of a shawl.

And no one,
not even you, my love,
will be able to part us.

Isle of Demons

The Isle of Demons is a small island in the Gulf of St Lawrence. According to legend, a young French noblewoman, niece to a governor of seventeenth-century New France and destined to join a religious order, was abandoned there after forming a liaison with a young officer during her voyage out.

Shipbound

At supper the young lieutenant
speaks of snowfields vaster
than this sea we cross – each tree
a cathedral. Even the birds,
he tells me,
sing in a foreign tongue.

I have not come this far
to hear birds sing. Force from me
strict music – teach me to heal
with bitter herbs, till they lick
Your honey from my hands.

I pray continuously for the ship to hasten
to that rough land where I will serve You
in clogs and coarse wool. Forgive my jewels,
stigmata of my uncle's pride. Absolve me
of these silks riding my skin
the way foam rides this sea we cut
but cannot mark.

The sailors tell how frost will sear the trees,
drown us in one long howl of fire. This land
breeds demons, more than there are beads
to choke them. Help me, Lord.
Save me from waters
salt or sweet –

Stop my uncle's tongue,
the stories of the young lieutenant,
all the sailor's lies. Seal my ears
with your white silence –

let me read
only the apothecary's jars:
basil, camomile and mint,
the pale, cut tongues of linden flowers.

The Young Lieutenant

is not as young as I believed. A wife, a small child
left behind. The young lieutenant is the younger son
of a younger son – he goes to take a holding
where the river lies against the land, he says
the way a woman's arm lies, bare,
along a table.

At table with his master, my uncle,
I sip water, drink the wine
of other stories. I tell myself
how, when the young lieutenant's sleigh
smashes the ice, when spears
tear his breast, I will heal him
at the Hôtel Dieu.

❀

Worse storms below, a roil
of sickness, stench.
He shows me how to seize
the railing, plunge
into each sucking gulf.

It is the calms you cannot guard against.

❀

My woman comes with ivory combs
to plait my hair – thick, black, she says
as a sky without stars. How deft her hands,
even as the deck swerves, combs
careening to the floor. When she coils
my hair she finds no mark
not even a shadow
on the skin between collar and nape.

His lips have crossed that sea as many times
as I have prayed for shipwreck;
through nights blind as my eyelids
he has dropped his hooks

to that earth under the waters
God parted with his breath.

Her Serving Woman's Lament

The Archangel Himself strikes so
and punishes.
He has made us devil's meat –

Hail Mary
now and in the hour

No mercy in men, nor wisdom.
Only the power a dog has over a bone.
Our cunning no match – stitching
slit silks, smoothing hair, splashing rose water.
It was the salt betrayed them, we couldn't scrub the salt
from her skin.

of our death

Such things happen while we have blood,
not sour wine within us, while flesh
mounts our bones and rides us hard.

pray for us sinners

Ordered each night to his table
she'd neither eat nor drink,
saving thirst and hunger for a finer feast.
Who then is governor? The one who banishes?
Or, lost inside the country of her breasts,
the one who plants his flag
between her thighs?

full of grace

The Island

Hatchets, needles,
tinder-box. Biscuit and salt pork enough
to last six weeks.
A crucifix we hold by turns,
shutting our hands
as if to make them innocent again.

Our seigneury: the Isle of Demons.
I have heard them singing fire
in the night, but now they sleep
silent as fog.

What you have done will kill your mother
a second time: poison your father's bread.
No penance strict enough save death. Your body
a sieve leaking sin and never empty.

My uncle rails, but grants this grace:
he will leave us to each other,
playing house in hell.

Saucepan and hunting knife.
A barrel for catching rain water: three
wooden bowls, three trenchers. He is not
unprovident, though my woman wrings
her hands and weeps. I bid her pull canvas
across rocks; gather kindling.
Brine enough in the wind.

Hunters

He leaves before light with a bow
fashioned from my ribs, a plait of my hair.
His arrows enter me:
the pores of my skin are beasts hid
in the fever of the trees.

This island abounds in fresh springs
and berries. Here are roots
we may eat, herbs I will brew to soothe
my young lieutenant, who no longer drinks
the moon from my breasts.
At night he calls out his wife's name,
his child's.

When my time comes
I'll rip a length from my skirt for swaddling;
fish lullabies up from the dark.

And still he'll leave to hunt
what he cannot find,
return with head hanging like the hares
whose necks he snaps.
No mark, not even a bruise
where his heart was.

The First Winter

My skin brown, hard as the runners
of a sledge. You can count
every bone – were he to run his hands the length
of me I would give out the sound of a fence
drubbed by a stick. Except for this belly
swelling under hunger's stone. We boil spruce bark,
chew leaves, melt snow to drink –
the whites of his eyes.

My woman tells her beads, over and over.
All day he hacks at trees,
dismembering, as if each branch
disgorged a demon.

Because of what roots in me
no ice can cloud my breath. I crouch at stream's edge
to hook fish; bring down birds with his bow.
His child swings from my bones
kicking my blood to broth.

All night my lieutenant lies white
against me, each snow-silent night.
Only in sleep can he cup himself round me, drink
and not break. My woman cups him,
making this trinity:
bone and flesh and breath.

Burial

If this land ever loosens,
if rock gives up even a fist of soil
we will dig him a space to cradle in –
he who will never hold his child.

I have stitched a shroud,
weighted it with stones
out of the shove of the wind.
Snow holds him now
day and night.

Demons

Hook-teeth, laughter
rips me, roots
of my hair to the lips he entered
like a whisper.

The rails I seize now
are my own bones.

His child spurts blue as silence.
My woman runs to the stream,
plunges crucifix and child
together. I cannot tell the cry
from ice, splintering.

Child or demon
sucking my breasts? Smashed plate
of afterbirth, heart's
famished river.

Summer

Miracles: that a child could suckle skeleton
yet grow to ripen in this sun.
That we have survived for this:
heat slapping our skins, the very air
grown fat. A feast of berries, so many
we crush them to each other's mouths, stained
with their sweet, good blood.

Our skin too tough for flies to pierce,
hair a better shield than those rags we burned.
At night we lie with the child between us,
locking legs and arms to cradle her.
So close we are always walking through
each other's dreams, spaces no wider
than gap between lid
and eye.

Names

The child as much hers
as mine. It is only fitting
they should lie together.

I could not tell whose breath
quit whose body first.

Stones to weight their eyes –
none to mark names.
They have no names, now;
earth erases them.

Through gaps in my teeth,
the gash between my lips,
I call my self: no
name.

The Captain's Report

Making landfall on the Isle of Demons we discovered traces
that were not wholly unexpected. Your Grace's conjectures
were accurate, except in one particular.

We spent three days on an island small enough to cross in a morning.
At dusk we retired to the ship, the men believing the lake
to be haunted by spirits. (I myself heard cries, doubtless
the call of some strange waterfowl.)

On the afternoon of the second day we found two graves marked
with sticks and what appeared to be hair. Black,
and fine, and long.

The third day, we were found. It seems she had been stalking us
from the start. I say 'she,' but be advised that the creature which
disclosed itself could not be called a woman. Hair hacked round
her head; eyes fixed, never falling. Her dugs and nether parts
she made no move to hide. As if she thought them no more
shame to her than hands or feet.

I cannot tell how long we looked on her, or she at us. But I know this:
though I held out my hand as if sweetmeats cradled there,
she would not move until I spoke – words fit for a child, a bird.
She approached, but would not speak, her tongue
a peg in the hole of her mouth.

I assure your Grace, she has been treated with the courtesy
her rank demands. Throughout the voyage she wanted for nothing

and received constant spiritual attention, much-needed
after the foulness for which she was thrust into that desert.

She suffered herself to be clothed in men's garments –
we had no others. Her hair cleaned,
her cracked feet shod, she was brought,
at last, to make confession. Grunts and howls.

Following Your Grace's instructions your niece has been left
with the Sisters of the Blessed Sacrament. Upon my last inquiry
I was informed that she is still not capable of speech,
and that, though perfectly docile, she does not comprehend
the nature of obedience.

Cellbound

The room ten paces
by fifteen. A cot, prie-dieu,
hooks on the wall,
one of them a crucifix.

I have been here as long
as it takes black hair
to become its own ghost. For my breasts
to hang themselves
from my ribs.

Night Eye

No one and nothing to see. This path I have never taken but know,
the way my blood knows my bones.

Night on night alone: a crying like calling. Demons, leaping
into the cauldron of their tongues.
Night on night I lie – husk without one seed to rattle.

Soles of my feet,
whorled ears to the Invisible

how the dark swarms
such honey it distills

my bones – twigs rafting the water – part
to let dark enter. My skin

steeps in it, even
the whites of my eyes.

Demons shaped like birds,
blank breasts, inked throats

diving, surging, calling me
by grief, by bliss

tongue and teeth,
music that roots me, roots me

a pod

       a husk

              black boat through shifting waters

III.

Marrying the Sea

for Michael

In Praise of Gravity

Lauritz Melchior,
the greatest Wagnerian tenor of his day,
walks out into his garden one afternoon
to practice scales.

Late spring, dandelions
haunting the grass, warm blizzards
of pear blossom, and Melchior
tilting his head back like a golden bowl.

The music makes a disturbance
in the atmosphere – not only birds and
balloons, mayflies, cigarette smoke, stray
scraps of paper whirl into the garden,
into the spectacle of this huge man
climbing
the silken ladder
of his voice –

not only birds and balloons but also
an aeroplane flying all day
back and forth over Copenhagen,
another aeroplane full of cameras behind it.
To Lauritz Melchior they are no more than
bluebottles buzzing, till

the belly of one plane opens like a pair of lips,
disclosing, delicate
as a lace handkerchief, a lady. As she falls
his voice achieves the purity
of astonishment.

Into the eddy of his song, cords
of her parachute thrumming,
Kleinchen drifts. Her feet
the swansdown of a powder puff, her hands
almond dragées that melt away
even as he kisses them.

Three months later, movie actress,
opera singer marry. Arm-in-arm,
they stroll their Tivoli of days and nights

in his breastpocket, a foam of lace;
octaves ringing
her every finger.

Marrying the Sea

Marriages work or don't
work out: dray horses, lapsed
exercise fanatics. Must be saved,
like stamps, rubber bands,
compost. You get in or out of them like cars,
never asking where they're supposed
to be taking you; whether
you've been stalled in the driveway
twenty minutes, twenty years.

Marriages must be maintained. Like lawns:
weeded, trimmed, never walked on. Must have
multiple blooms; be disease-resistant, colourful,
and above all, fragrant – the most desirable of roses.

Marriages – ever-looming
Everests of dirty underwear
or diapers, telephone
and power bills. And up this Everest,
Desire toils, a small,
pale figure unequipped
with oxygen. Each year
smaller, paler,
slower.

❀

Sometimes, when I count up
how many of our friends are undivorced,
it's hard to keep from touching wood, even

paper will do. Sometimes – when we kiss
in a cinema or on a street in the wide-
open afternoon; kiss as though our hearts
have leaped into our tongues –

I can hear people thinking
Marital Exhibitionists!
When, after a few week's separation, we rush
headlong to each other, I can't help but wonder:
are we phoenixes, or simply slaves
of that sluggard, habit?

Perhaps, during that ceremony all those
years ago, something in the veils and incense
didn't take, freeing us
from our wedding poses,
making us fluid, unstable
as the greens and blues of our photos.

Or was it that storm of waves
where we honeymooned
at Monterosso al Mare? You plunging in
again and again, while I hugged shore,
staring at the masts of fishing boats
and campaniles, until I fell
in a slam of water. My arms
no stronger than my hair, my dress

as the sea sucked from my finger
the ring we'd never thought to,
could never have afforded to insure.

Not money but a talisman we searched for
all the remaining days: fingers
scrabbling through sand,
throwing up impromptu castles –
abandoned, like the shore
we couldn't keep from altering.

Those times when we are most at one;
when we make of our joined selves
a breakwater, holding everything we are
against everything that would dissolve us,

I think of that ring,
its small diamond, the too-bright gold
tumbling from my finger
with an acrobat's risky grace.

Think of it empty, endlessly
embracing, marrying
the sea.

Sweet Tooth

... many say that sugar is mild, but to me sugar is violent, and I call it so.
— Roland Barthes, *Camera Lucida*

1. Once, in a foreign city,
    we quarrelled over a slice of cake.
    It was not that I thought you greedy;
    it was not that we couldn't afford it, that the cake
    was stale, the icing blowzy –
    it was all these, and it was only
    that you desired what I didn't.

    Wanting us always only
    to want together, I left you
    with your mouth full of sugar;
    blazed from the restaurant, my tongue
    sprung like a Swiss army knife.

    Pacing an alleyway, I divorced you,
    disburdened myself a thousand times,
    till it was almost too late to rush to the concert hall
    and find you, as if by accident, in the seat beside me.

    The musicians struck up *Verklärte Nacht*. You remained
    aloof. Halfway through I had to keep myself
    from clutching your hand instead of the programme.
    Suddenly all I wanted was you, whether you wanted me

    or not. Because you didn't want me it was all I could do
    not to kiss you till your teeth cracked, till walls,
    music, everyone around us burst
    like sugar in a splash of boiling water.

88

2. We didn't have the kind of wedding cake
    stacked in bakery windows: doll bride,
    doll groom, battlements
    of iced cardboard

    but a Ukrainian wedding bread: golden,
    studded with clove-eyed doves. My grandmother
    played magician, pulling wings
    from sleeves of dough.

    There was fruitcake
    for the English guests – denser
    than chocolate, entombed
    in icing.

    Two of the doves still roost
    in my mother's freezer, frost
    singeing their wings. The cake
    was eaten long ago, yet
    when we get caught in the machinery
    of marriage, it haunts us still:

    that dark split by a silver knife;
    the smell of burnt sugar.

No se puede vivir sin amar

No trees,
woodcutters gone crazy
or missing.
If I were Red Riding Hood
would you unzip me with an axe?

Vagaries, constancy,
what's for dinner tonight?
Lovemaking in autumn fields,
portable jambalaya.

While the dog sucks burrs
out of his dinner jacket, I dream
we're in bed together with a third party;
he puts his hand on my breast,
underdone egg yolk, squealing all
over the plate.

What you dream you never tell me
censors in ten-sizes-too-big-
trenchcoats, axeing livewood.

Across the one-eyed night
a black wicker of branches. Your face, mine
strange as knuckles, kneecaps, everything unknown.

Children

A street party downtown, our own neighbourhood.
All the doors open, tables with Christmas
stockings, papier mâché pumpkins, midsummer
night's garlands, small white eyes hiding in the leaves.

Why did our invitations never arrive? We shake out silks,
rummage closets for outrageous hats.
Through fevers of preparation a clock chimes:
too late, too early, now, never. Just as we step out

the street dissolves. No houses, swingsets,
shade trees, garages. Just sand sifted with basalt.
Holding the stones of each other's hands, nowhere
to sit with our grief – grit worrying our hair and skin,
a stubborn, sudden gravity.

Into this desolation, like vees of migrating birds,
voices of children. Somewhere there must be water,
for they appear carrying buckets, shovels,
small boats with canvas sails.

Without being told, they pick up our debris,
make no reproach that we'd forgotten them. Where they dig,
palm trees and pyramids seed: the mouths of oases.

Nobody's dream, these children, they are real.

Questions We Are Not Supposed to Ask

Out of the blue, àpropos
of nothing, I ask
How important to you is sex?
I think you are going to leap to a reply
but you hold back, as though something
warm and delicate were in your mouth:
a newborn kitten, an unhatched egg.
Love, you say, at last.
Love is the most important thing in the world to me.

Love, of course. But where does that leave us?
One could easily separate the two;
Kundera's arch-philanderers do it all the time,
wives in this bowl, mistresses in that,
as if what they were making were soufflé.
But you are no chef: you were thinking of some global
homecoming: our children, our aged parents,
and the aged parents we'll become, all
gathered in love's ample house. No one
left out begging in the street.

I'm talking of married love, that dance
to the music of familiarity. To ask
for desire to last as long as love –
why not ask for the moon?
I do ask: not for pleasures stashed
like sweets in a bag,
but simply to keep on wanting what we have.

Kundera, again, his aesthetics
of perpetual surprise. How to make marriage
into poetry? Our first argument, when I slapped your face
and you dropped, one by one, ice cubes
down my back, and it was not funny.
It was the ground flooding open

floor flush with water, glass –
ruins of that aquarium where love had flicked
prettily, back and forth.

How many times since
have we surprised each other?
– highboard dives that brought the whole
house down. And what's love, our love,
but an old tin tub? Big-bellied, sometimes overflowing
yet still unbroken. Room for two,
whatever waters surge between them.

High dives into bathtubs: not
the most exalted metaphor,
but it will do, love,
it will have to do.

Roses, roses

I

Agog.
An armful of the best
red roses, and not even from a lover –
a husband!

I hold them like a newborn,
supporting the soft, unfinished head.

II

From a glass coffee pot on my desk
a faint tinnitus of scent,

dark, respectful enough
for a dowager queen. Just unfolding, but
their redness seasoned,

as if infused with black; as if,
on a bright day, your shadow were to walk
through the wall of your skin, and embrace you.

III

How to tell these roses:
tart, blood-tongued kisses.

Oh, their scent is a rain of arrows –
I am Saint Sebastian with twelve archers
aiming again and again: Saint Sebastian
in a Saint Teresa swoon –

They smell like mulberries taste,
more complicated than other fruit;
the down on their lips so plush
you could graze them forever.

IV

Shameful. The showiness,
the expense. Floral equivalent
of mink stoles and cadillacs

(alostroemeria is visually
more interesting
and lasts far longer).

Each petal heavy as a doorstop.
The whole ensemble a waiting room, crammed
with overstuffed settees:

nothing
but walk-ons, understudies,
excuses.

V

Part of me – the one with an expansive
private income, never needing to worry
about mortgage payments, electricity bills –
is ravished,

cannot look at the roses
without thinking of your tongue
travelling my skin.

VI

Flibbertigibbets –
they chatter all night
while I'm trying to sleep,
wave hands red
as a washer-woman's.

Loosening corsets, letting down
their scrolled-up hair, they're bad

as a convention of Toulouse-Lautrec
madames. What's to be done with
all this abandon?

The refrigerator gives them gooseflesh,
they're calling for flannel nightgowns,

but I sleep a long way from any kitchen.

VII

Huddled in shawls,
they lean out from their balcony
into the slow warmth of morning.

Silky whispers
of their hearts: *let us out,*
let us out.

Innocent, golden, contrived:
like the pea
bruising the twelve-mattressed princess.

VIII

Fountains, *feux de joie.*
Bud-sheaths doing the splits:
green gams burst
by so much bloom.

All day, even while I'm out, they go
on.

IX

Now that the petals have begun to stoop
I learn to appreciate the leaves:
they knock back quarts of light.

Like short, stocky men
who marry tall, beautiful women:
rich men; hungry women.

X

One, two – heads down, broken-necked,
leaves prematurely
huddled. Prisoners, forbidden water.

This is the worst of roses, the something meaty
in their bloom.

Tulips only wither, you find their twisted smiles
on the breakfast table,
bald, bug-eyed stems
loitering in the water. But these –

I've removed one, discreetly, the way
in some hotels, they wheel out
guests who die in the night.

I hang it upside down on the wall:
floral pietà.

XI

Each morning more
and more limp flags. I shake them,

disclose the shock of pollen at a centre
violated just in being open. A small bush,
brassy not even gold.

At last I perform the customary rites:
lay out the bodies, tie ribbon round their heels,
hang them from a cupboard hook.

Air's buzzard mouth
eats them.

XII

What I know of roses
is what I know of our hearts.
That they're muscled,
mortal.

Leave the silk, the paper, the plastic
to their petrified bloom. Let the roses flower,
perish. Long after they've leached
into dump or compost – red ghosts
flaring round us. Incandescence.

Ithaka

On the drive up, trying to fend off
this brute tumult of mountains, I phoned home
in my head. Making sure home wasn't mythical:
you and our sons at the kitchen table,
the dog flopped on the rug, by the radio.

This separation is temporary,
an exchange of hills and small river
for this rage of water, sky crammed with rock.

My nights here will be avalanches,
snow plugging my throat
while you sleep in our bed,
our bed huge and whole as a planet.
Does my body still haunt the sheets, make its lair
where our legs tangled deeper than tree roots?

Something you once said about Odysseus, Penelope,
that olive tree making a pillar for their bed.
Even a sea nymph's vow to make him ageless as water
couldn't hold him, wanting only this:
to sleep in the arms of home.

How can I know what will happen, now
or when I return? How many islands
in these mountains, how many suitors at your door?
Will the dog thump his tail

in the threshold dust for me? Who will remember
my scars?

Bow's embrace
of the string. Arrows singing us
through and through.

Gathering Lilies
Photograph, 1894

A rowboat courting the slow,
sleek body of the river.

The boat catches
in the river's throat:
the river is whispering *lilies, lilies.*

She reaches out, her arms
gloved suddenly in cream, in gold,
tugging slimed stems from
mud-blind root.

In his hands the oars are
supple as reins.
He is thinking how the boat is shaped
like the curve of a waiting hand.

More and more lilies, warm
bowls, the very skin of light. The faces
of these lovers not yet turned to one another:
blood beating dark between them.

Meeting by Water

Out of this maze of streets a stranger walks toward me.
Unpremeditated yet expected, he has perfect manners
and a pair of wings, dwarfed, misshapen,
clotting the place where his heart should be.

Together we walk to a bridge over a great river.
We do not cross but stand looking down
at the drifting boats, at streetlamps sunk
like eclipsed moons.

I open my coat and show him my birthmark:
a wattled stain, coloured like blood stirred
into mud. He puts his mouth to my breasts;
the stain is wine, pours clear away.

When I touch them, his wings become wishbones,
break apart. Now there is nothing between us.
We stay on the bridge a long time,
arms round one another, eyes closed

as the river rises. It carries us off,
together, in different directions.
Everything solid has vanished.
The air fills with a smoke like rain.

Jealous

of the deaf-mute woman in the Thai restaurant,
her beautifully plain, worn face,
even her track suit.
Of your giving her five dollars for her pamphlet,
The Deaf-Mute Alphabet.
Her ecstasy of surprise.

❧

Of the straw-blonde bottle of grappa
on your computer table. Of the window holding
your Turin-shroud face, at midnight, over the screen.

❧

Of the students of either sex and every age
who line up at the confessional of your office.
The tenderness with which you hear them out,
the loans of Dollimore, Kosofsky Sedgwick, Slavoj Zizek.

❧

Of the dog when he pushes his black-starred muzzle
into your hand, and it perfectly fits. Of the time you spend
hunting fleas from his coat, though someone has to do it
and I won't.

❧

Of your obsession with viol music after seeing
Tous les Matins du Monde. Your secret
asceticism.

❧

Of your rogue's gallery of chums: Hermes
Trismegistus, Johannes Trithemius,
Descartes in his melon-dreaming days.
Cornelius Agrippa of Nettesheim.

❧

Of your rapturous abstraction, book
in hand, everyday-soup boiling over.
The selflessness of such abstraction,
the pure grain of that wood.

❧

Of how cleanly you skate: swift, sinewy curves
over the roughest ice. How, when I'm dumpy in down
you need only a sweater; thaw my hands with your breath,
give me your gloves to wear over mine.

❧

Of your needing no such subterfuge,
no filters, no back-handed trope
to name what you love.

❀

Of how you belong to yourself.

Of books with your name inscribed.

Of our sons keeping you sketched in their genes.

Of earth in whose arms you'll lie without turning.

Of the photographs that will never lose your face.

Making Strange

Sometimes I look out the kitchen window,
and where the badminton net's strung, see
that affair I never had when we were first married

or, in the peonies,
three red-haired daughters, their skin
the same spiced white of peony flowers.

What if, new-married, guilty
at so much unearned happiness,
I'd run off with a one-eyed lover, or
met him over a whole winter in a secret
Bloomsbury boarding house?

Say he was Australian, and a convert
to Islam. Would I have spent
hours making soft cages
out of black crêpe?
Scented all my baths with
eucalyptus oil?

The badminton net is torn,
its poles stagger away from each other.
Meaning unspeakable grief? Or just the long
scritch of a sheet being torn
to fit two different beds, two
separate houses?

Years later, in a foreign city, would I recognize
in that man feeding gulls by a canal
the husband I'd abandoned?

I'd want to call out, but my voice
would be lost in a white ruckus.
He wouldn't stay long, but walk off
to an appointment, or to lunch with his wife.
I would stand with my hands
in my pockets, then turn away –

to an empty hotel room?
To the theatre where I will meet my three
red-haired daughters for a matinée?

On the wall above the window
Marina Tsvetayeva's face, each beautiful eye
a globe of sadness.
Falling in love, she says
is not like walking on water.

A Book of Hours

We had a huge house downtown, too full
of furniture and people. Crowds on the window sills
and thronging the beds. They call for bean soup,
ashtrays, we run up and down stairs, trays turning
to playground slides, all the windows steaming up
with smoke. At last your bare arm brushes against my lips;
I bite down, making a small wound that has
to be attended to. Once alone in the dispensary
(the same one in which Lara irons in *Dr. Zhivago*)
you part my thighs as if they are wings.

❀

Walking in the magenta of twilight, we discover,
in a spruce grove by the sea, a house we never knew
existed. Empty of everything, it enchants us;
we stretch out on bare bookshelves lining the walls,
find ourselves travelling together through Egdon Heath,
the Lake District, Akhmatova's gardens in Tsarskoe Selo.
We walk for days through nights and into days again,
pockets full of bread, wineskins bulging at our sides,
taking shelter in empty houses, in spruce groves by the sea.

❀

I run away from home to the West Edmonton Mall.
I'm tired of cooking, steam from the pots has bleached
all our paintings pale as saltines. Inside the mall
I step on an escalator that turns into a cage like the ones

on construction sites; it jerks up and up, to where
the oxygen begins to thin. I can barely shout
to the solitary passer-by, a man with a hat like a green
apple. He returns with you, you're in your dressing gown
and were reading in bed. I can just make out the title,
The Unfortunate Traveller, sticking out your pocket.
You reach up your hand as if conducting *Lohengrin* –
I descend in stages fine as the breastfeathers
of an eider duck.

Invited to London for some royal occasion, a jubilee
or coronation, we settle into our Palace rooms,
arranging lilacs in the duvet, cigars under the pillow.
Outside, a troop of Don Cossacks, pursued by borzois,
tears up the grass. An act of homage, you explain,
stropping an old-fashioned razor purchased for the occasion.
The bathtub is big as the Titanic, by the time I swim back
the bedroom is dark, silent, except for the green grin
of a clock radio; it plays a medley from *Oklahoma*!
sung by Kiri te Kanawa and Tom Waits. Twelve hours later,
you return with a slice of fruitcake wrapped in a napkin.
It was, you explain, a wedding: *Charles and Camilla*
in silver ink, the finest calligraphy. I take the cake,
unwrap it from the cellophane, place it with the lilacs
in the bidet. It dissolves to potting soil.

After putting the children to bed, I leave the house
and walk along the shore to town. It's evening,
late spring, and would be pleasant except for the jab
of my sharp, thin heels, long as drinking straws.
At last I find the place I'm looking for; it takes
a long time to struggle up the dunes to the front door.
The man who opens it is the colour of cocoa, I put out
my hands to catch the steam rising from his skin.
His house is a collage of papers and tabletops,
a Braque still life. I glimpse you in a corner;
you make a sideways motion with your hand, and go on
talking to the man, who's put on a green eye shade.
There's no extra chair, so I take off my shoes and sit
on the floor. You talk and talk, a small black dog
whines at the kitchen door, no one's going to let him out
but me. I don't mean to leave, but the night's
Baltic-blue and the waves toss themselves like courtesans'
petticoats on the shore. Halfway down, I realize
I've left my shoes behind; if it weren't for a brown
paper bag on a nearby rock, I'd be in a pretty pickle.
Inside the bag are a pair of shoes, buckled,
with small, curved heels. The kind of shoes
Katherine Mansfield would have worn to dinner
at the Woolfs'. Inside the shoes, a note from you:
How beautiful are the feet.

You are killed on a solo camping trip. I drive up
to Algonquin, wiping my eyes as if they're the windshield,
streaming. Once past the gates, everything is green glass
and grey glass: trees, sky, lake. Not even the loons
can break it, though I see, on the surface of the water,
long marks of their cries like tracks left by skaters.
A short, gruff man in a hunting jacket sits in the bow
of a canoe; he's my guide to the island where your body
lies caught between rocks at the base of a cliff. He says
you were out walking at night when you shouldn't have been.
The man wants to make love with me, here in the canoe,
his rough, stump hands so unlike yours, everything about him
unlike you *I can't* I say over and over *I can't*. From the rocks
you walk down to us, you've seen nothing, you drag
the canoe onto shore, offer your hand to help me out.
We're alone now, walking silently into the heart
of the island, past pines, moss, sleeves of rotting birch,
onto a plain of dunes and tall, sad reeds. You tell me
there's someone else, you are filled with sorrow
and newness. We walk and walk, nothing I can say
can win you back. At last you bow your head,
return to shore, and leaving the canoe for me,
swim farther and farther away. Your strokes so sharp
they score the glass.

On your way to work one morning, you disappear
and I go looking all over the wide world for you,
acting in shabby theatres, music halls, to pay the cost
of my ticket. Years go by, until at last, walking down
a *calle* in Venice one winter night, a *calle* just off
the *Fondamente Nuovo*, I look into the lighted window
of a print shop to see the back of a tall,
emaciated man. He's holding a page up to a lamp;
it's one of the original illustrations to *Pinocchio*. I stand
stamping my feet on the pavement, willing myself to walk
on, to stop imagining the tall, emaciated man to be you,
since I know that in a moment he will turn and show
a stranger's face. My longing is a bottle of dark, red wine.
I have never drunk from it, nor sucked the barley-sugar
trapping lint in my pockets. I force myself to walk on,
but suddenly I'm walking inside, so stealthily the man
can't hear and turn round. I put the wine and sugar
on a workbench; I walk to the man, stretch out my hands
and he turns to me. A face starred by little scars,
the kind made by a candle lit over the sleeping body
of a lover. I hold your head to my breast, you part
the wings of my thighs. Light streams,
careless, into the dark.

Dig

Letters, concert programmes, recipes,
hospital bracelets worn by our newborns,
immunization records, cancelled passports – the matter
of living together in love.

Archaeologists work with the beautiful hands of daylight
on their shoulders. Digging down to the last place anything human
moved or was touched. Where all we can possibly know ends.

But we begin together in the dark we mistook for day – everything
we had yet to learn about each other. From that place the layers rise.
Migrations from house to house, across seas, and a sea of highways.
Separations, absences even when sleeping side by side. And joy
like the gold of ancient diadems, bright after centuries in earth.

Layer after layer, we dig up to where love gives out:
where we must break, alone, into the emptiness of light.

Adoration of the Mystic Lamb

I believe in an afterlife:
paradise with icons, desires
promiscuously mixed. I believe you and I
will be together after our deaths,
in a place distant and foreknown:
those green uplands painted by Van Eyck
for the altar of St Bavo's Church, in Ghent. Cliffs and gorges,
caparisoned knights, ladies lifting martyr-palms long,
delicate as insect feelers.

I have worked out all the complications.
Whoever dies first will take up residence
in a niche shaped like a halved cocoon.
Waiting in our supple, golden skin,
we won't be bored, listening
to angels with clear contracted eyes
making fierce harmony.

The air will be braided with their music,
braided like egg challah, but we won't need to eat,
only to listen and look out.
We'll wait, not without impatience,
but in no distress: one hand raised as if in greeting,
the other gently cupping our sex,
the way we'd touch the faces of our small,
sleeping children, to make sure
they were still breathing.

The moment we sight one another
is the moment the floor gives way.
Instead of falling, we hover.
Below us there's a huge, serendipitous party,
a jamboree, with everyone
we've ever known or loved, or wanted to.

They're aware of us in the air above:
how the intertwining of our legs and arms,
our tongues and fingers makes all waving,
calling out, impossible. And so we fly
over their heads and that altar like a red steamer trunk,
on which the Mystic Lamb is telling a long, sheepish joke.

In town, our parents are fixing
tea or a pot of borscht. As we drift, enmeshed,
between tree tops and ether, they call out to us:
– *we've checked on the kids and they're fine* –

We are already sailing back to them,
and we are setting out, never
to return. We have vanished,
and can still be seen by anyone

looking out for us
with the eyes of love.

Notes and Acknowledgements

Sacra Conversazione is a term used to describe those paintings of the Renaissance in which one or two saints are shown conversing on sacred subjects with the Virgin and Child: speech so intense it achieves the fullness of silence.

Wind voller Weltraum: wind full of infinite spaces. Rainer Maria Rilke, 'The First Elegy,' *Duino Elegies*.

No se puede vivir sin amar: you can't live without loving. Malcolm Lowry, *Under the Volcano*.

❀

Many thanks for their fine and careful readings of this book to Clare Goulet, Michael Keefer, Tim Lilburn, Esta Spalding and to Jan Zwicky, peerless editor.

A salute to Bob, Jacquie, Maureen, Maury, Paul, Susan and Sylvia, who were all a part of its making, as was St Peter's Abbey, Muenster, Saskatchewan.

Computer help from Peter Brigg and Maury Wrobleski gratefully acknowledged.

I wish to thank Gilda Oliver for her generosity in allowing me to use her extraordinary sculptures for the covers of this book.

❀

Some of these poems have appeared in different versions in *The American Voice, Canadian Forum, event, The Fiddlehead, Grain, The Malahat Review, McGill Street Magazine, Poetry Canada Review* and *The New Quarterly.*

RUTH KAPLAN

About the Author

Janice Kulyk Keefer is the author of nine books of poetry, fiction and literary criticism, and a contributor to numerous anthologies. She has twice been nominated for a Governor General's Award, and twice won first prize in both the CBC Radio Literary Competition and the National Magazine Awards. *Travelling Ladies* was one of ten works of fiction chosen for *Ms.* magazine's International Fiction List; her newest novel, *The Green Library*, was nominated for a Governor General's Award and will shortly be published in Germany. She teaches at the University of Guelph and lives in Eden Mills, Ontario.